Mo Vaughn

ANGEL ON A MISSION

by

Mike Shalin

SPORTS PUBLISHING INC.

www.SportsPublishingInc.com

Book design, editor: Susan M. McKinney
Cover design: Scot Muncaster
Photos: *The Associated Press,* Trinity Pawling and Seton Hall University.

ISBN: 1-58261-046-0
Library of Congress Catalog Card Number: 99-64073

SPORTS PUBLISHING INC.
SportsPublishingInc.com

Printed in the United States.

Contents

Mo addresses the media at the press conference announcing his signing with the Anaheim Angels.
(AP/Wide World Photos)

CHAPTER ONE

Goodbye to Boston

Christmas, 1998, came a month early for Anaheim Angels manager Terry Collins—in a package that would hardly fit under the family tree.

"He's one of those guys who makes a team better in a lot of ways," Collins said after learning Mo Vaughn would be his new first baseman. "He gives us that big horse in the middle of the lineup and that takes some of the pressure off the other guys. We still have a lot of young players who were suddenly on the firing line in September. He is not

Mo takes a look around during his first day of spring training with the Angels. (AP/Wide World Photos)

afraid to stand up and say, 'let's not be intimidated, we're as good as anybody.

"Leadership in the clubhouse is very important if done the right way. He prepares right and plays right. He carries credibility."

That was the general feeling around baseball about Maurice Samuel Vaughn, the 31-year-old first baseman—of the Anaheim Angels?

The sound of Mo's name being linked to any team except the Red Sox was hard to digest for fans in New England or around baseball, where Mo was perceived as being the Boston Red Sox. Even when it looked as if a deal wouldn't work out between Mo and the Sox, there was always a feeling of, "ah, he'll go back to Boston. That's where he belongs."

Sox fans had watched players like Carlton Fisk, Fred Lynn and Roger Clemens be allowed to walk away, two of them going on to continue Hall of Fame careers. There was no way it could happen again.

Mo was an important leader with the Red Sox. (AP/Wide World Photos)

But it did—after really what amounted to years of harsh negotiations and shots fired back and forth, Mo Vaughn was gone. The Red Sox had lost their first baseman, lost their leader—and, perhaps most important, lost that credibility Collins mentioned. The whole thing didn't make sense.

It all ended in a rather strange way, too. Two weeks or so before the Angels signed Vaughn to a six-year deal worth a guaranteed $80 million, with an option for a seventh year (the richest deal in baseball until Kevin Brown's Dodger contract topped it a month later), Vaughn stood in front of his house in Easton, Massachusetts, on a chilly night and told WBZ-TV's Steve Burton the Red Sox would have a new first baseman in 1999.

"Best wishes to the Boston Red Sox and their fans because I understand your intensity and what you want," Mo said that night. "I tried to bring that and I have no regrets. I don't know what's going to happen in my situation yet. My family and I decided this is the best thing to do.

"I'll miss (Boston). I've done a lot of things here with the kids. I've done a lot of things in this city and I'll continue. So, it will always be within me, and I'll always remember the good times, and the bad times taught me some things. It was overall a great eight years. I don't look back in a negative way at all."

Mo was in the process of leaving Boston in his rear-view mirror. A home-grown talent after being drafted by the Red Sox out of Seton Hall University, the New England native was moving west. Perhaps it was fitting he would sign with the Disney folks - his career to that point was kind of a fairy tale, with all the strange twists you expect from the movie maker.

"This is obviously a huge day for the organization," said Angels general manager Bill Bavasi—

after signing the team's most significant free agent since Reggie Jackson in 1981. "We've never been afraid to go into the market. We've always been careful about what we do. There's a change in action. I don't believe we've seen the players who were the right fit. Guys like this don't come around very often."

In 1999, Mo Vaughn was set to be the highest-paid hitter in the major leagues. The road that got him to that point—and to the West Coast instead of the East—wasn't an easy one. In fact, it was filled with doubt—about his body, about his defense, about his strikeouts, about his outspokenness. There was, however, never any doubt about his talent or his desire to compete.

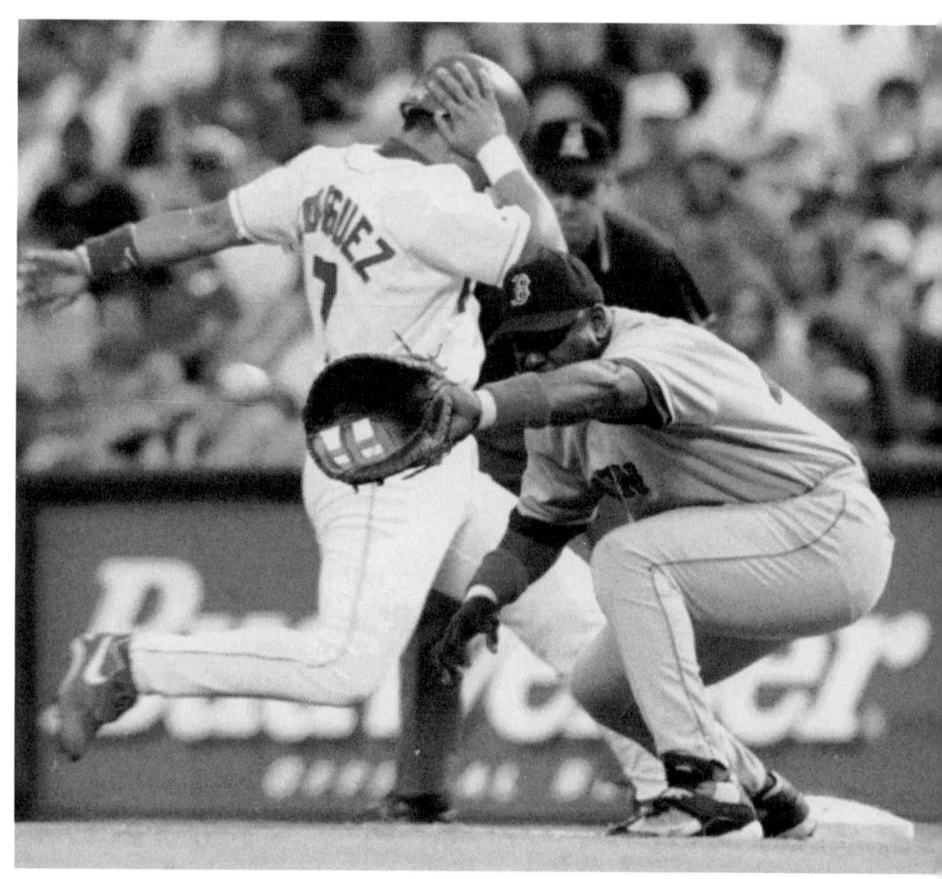

Mo played eight seasons in Boston. (AP/Wide World Photos)

CHAPTER TWO

You Could Tell Early

Baseball observers had noticed very early in Mo's career that there was something special about him.

"Watching him from his rookie season," said Bavasi, "this guy at a very young age took a leadership role. One thing that was important from my point of view was how his teammates feed off him. He's got natural ability. I know that. He has certain limitations he has to overcome. If I take it down to one word, it's leadership."

There is an old expression that says wisdom is

Mo (#30) was a football player at Trinity Pawling Prep School in New York. (Trinity Pawling).

born of pain. This never came easily for Mo, who is built more like a football linebacker than a first baseman. He could always hit, but those questions surrounding his defense and his ability to stay in shape haunted him through his early years in the game.

Every day, he went out and took ground balls with the hope of getting better at his position. For a time, he shed the big first baseman's mitt and worked at first before games wearing a kid's regular position glove, taking the pounding on his big left hand. Until the couple of years that led to his monster contract, he still was barely adequate in the field. Oh, did Mo ever have his painful moments out there. Missed grounders, missed throws, bad throws of his own. Nothing was more agonizing than a day in Detroit early in his career—the day Mo looked like he wanted to quit baseball. It also was the day that perhaps made him the man he is today.

Anyone at Tiger Stadium that Saturday afternoon will never forget what happened. Tim Naehring charged a slow roller that would have been turned into the final out—if Mo could just catch the throw. Simple-enough task, right? Wrong. Mo missed the throw, the ball went down the right field line and the Red Sox lost the game.

Later, as his teammates showered and dressed in the cramped locker room, Mo sat outside, in the dugout, alone in the pain of what had just happened. In the tiny manager's office, Butch Hobson, who had been with Mo in the minor leagues, never referred to his player as anything but, "the first baseman," as in, "the first baseman should have caught the ball." It was as if they'd never met.

Mo remained in the dugout for 30 minutes before John Valentin, his long-time friend and college teammate at Seton Hall, went out to console him and bring him inside.

Later that night, at a team gathering at a local hotel, Mo and Hobson had a confrontation. Depending on which witness was talking, it was anything from a verbal battle to a real brawl.

Regardless, Mo grew up a little that day—and the upbringing of Leroy and Shirley Vaughn of Norwalk, Connecticut, helped turn a floundering package of potential into a star—and the highest-paid player in the game.

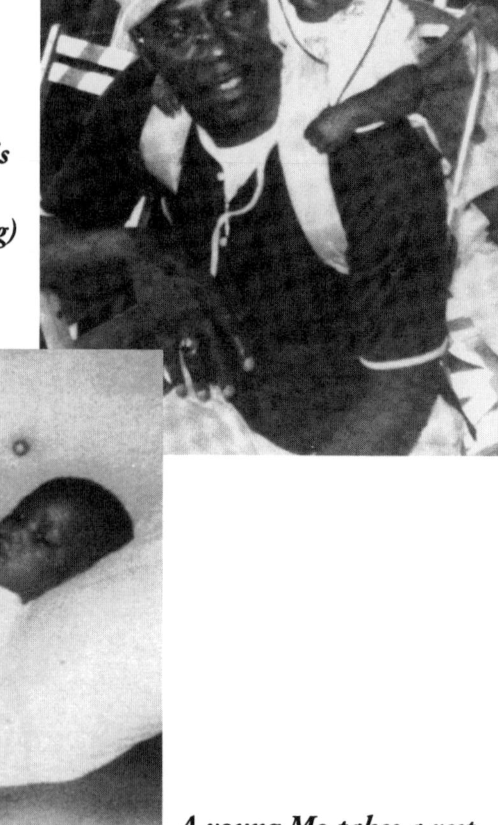

In his yearbook, Mo called his father, Leroy, his "best fan." (Trinity Pawling)

A young Mo takes a rest. (Trinity Pawling)

CHAPTER THREE

On His Way to Stardom

Like any kid, Mo could have messed up his life and amounted to nothing. If that had happened, there would have been no family reasons to blame. Mo's parents were both educators and one of his two sisters went on to become a teacher. Mo didn't love school ("I didn't like school at all," he would say later), probably the main reason his folks sent him to Trinity Pawling Prep in Pawling, N.Y., an all-boys boarding school where Mo, who needed the more structured setup to mature, spent three years laying the foundation for

While attending Trinity Pawling Prep School, Mo played football and basketball as well as baseball. (Trinity Pawling)

what would happen in the future.

He played baseball, football and basketball at Pawling, but it was clear baseball was his first love. In his book, "Mo Vaughn, Follow Your Dreams," Mo points out it was his mom who started him on his way—taking him into the backyard at age 3 and teaching her son how to hit, using a ball swinging from a tree on a rope.

"To this day, Mom gives me advice on how to hit," Mo said. "And, do you know what? She's usually right!" Mo hits lefthanded, because, as he once said, his mother only knew one way to put his hands on his bat.

From Pawling, Mo headed to Seton Hall University in New Jersey, where he set school records for homers and was named Big East Player of the Decade. He was selected in the fifth round of the 1986 draft by the Phillies out of high school, but Mom said he was going to college. Off he went. He

Mo set records for homers at Seton Hall. (Seton Hall)

later was taken by the Red Sox in the first round of the 1989 draft. This kid who grew up a Yankee fan (in awe when he went to Yankee Stadium) was going to play for the Red Sox.

The Phillies drafted Mo out of high school, but he went to college instead. (Seton Hall)

CHAPTER FOUR

Making the Short Jump to the Big Time

Red Sox fans, always starved for super stars, couldn't wait for Mo's arrival. In two years in the minor leagues, he did well enough to convince people he might turn into a quality major-leaguer.

In 1989, playing at Double A New Britain in his home state of Connecticut, Mo hit .278 in 73 games—but showed his potential by hitting eight homers and driving in 38 runs in a tough hitters' park.

It wasn't spectacular, but it was a good beginning for his professional career. Mo also played in the Florida Instructional League after the season and was the co-winner of the organization's Tony Latham Award, which goes to the player or players who show the most enthusiasm during the Instructional League season.

The following year, at hitter-friendly McCoy Stadium in Pawtucket, Rhode Island, Mo batted .295, 22 homers and 72 RBIs playing for the Triple A PawSox—just 45 minutes (depending on traffic) from Fenway Park.

Mo's season did not start out well. A left-handed pitcher, Shawn Barton, broke Mo's right hand with a pitch April 30 and Mo was out until June 5. When he returned, Mo, who had been struggling when he got hurt, continued to flounder, going just 2-for-23. After 26 total games, he was hitting just .161 in Triple-A and there was concern throughout the organization. Mo caught fire after that, hitting .338 with 17 homers and 59 RBIs over his last 82

Mo was drafted by the Red Sox in 1989. (AP/Wide World Photos)

games—and hitting safely in 44 of his last 54, batting .359 over that span.

In his first 181 games of pro baseball, Mo hit 32 homers. The other statistics that quickly were picked up by scouts and other team officials, however, was that he had struck out 134 times and made 21 errors. He led Eastern League first basemen in errors in 1989, making 10 in 73 games. None of this was unusual for a slugger trying to find the feel at the plate—a marked man seeing a steady diet of breaking stuff from pitchers afraid to give him fastballs. Word was there were "holes" in Mo's swing—again, nothing really unusual for a young power hitter trying to find his way. This was a young hitter who clearly had the potential to be one of the exciting bats in the game.

"Mo takes that big, healthy cut, where people say, 'If he'd hit that one it would have gone 500 feet,'" said Hobson.

CHAPTER FIVE

The First Call

Red Sox great Carl Yastrzemski recognized the hype surrounding Mo at spring training, 1991. "I know exactly what he's going through," Yaz said. "He came up with the big reputation just like me following Ted Williams. The pitchers are going right after him. I feel for him."

Said Mo: "They are pitching me like I've been in the league 10 years."

A disappointed Mo started the 1991 season at Pawtucket, where he hit .274, with 14 homers and

50 RBIs—including 13 homers in one 39-game span. It was clear by this time the power was there. It was time for a call to the big leagues and that call came June 27, when the Red Sox sent Phil Plantier to Triple-A to make room for Mo. Mo got word he was heading for the major leagues when his then-Pawtucket manager, Hobson, called him to his hotel room after midnight.

"I thought he was going to reprimand me," Vaughn said later. No reprimand. "I've won this hurdle, getting to the big leagues," Mo said. "Now I've got to stay."

Mo's first hit, a single, came the next day—off future teammate Todd Frohwirth. His first major-league homer, hit in his fourth game, June 30, was a titanic blast off the Orioles' Jeff Robinson at Baltimore's Memorial Stadium, going 438 feet and coming within a matter of rows of being the second ball ever hit completely out of that stadium.

Mo's first home run at Fenway Park came on July 4, 1991. (AP/Wide World Photos)

Frank Robinson, the Hall of Famer who hit the one that did go out, was in attendance that day and waved a towel at Mo in salute.

The next day, July 1, in Milwaukee, Mo hit one 435 feet off Jaime Navarro and drove in four runs. On July 4, Mo hit his first Fenway homer. He began his major league career by hitting .318 in his first 12 games. The hot start didn't last, however, and Mo slumped to a .246 average over the last 66 games and hit only one homer in his last 62 games.

As pitchers decided there was no reason to throw this young slugger fastballs near the plate, Mo suffered through streaks of 0-for-19 and 0-for-12. The "hole" theory was making the rounds again.

"Everyone kept saying he was the next Babe Ruth," said his manager, Joe Morgan. "It doesn't work out that way. Not very often, anyway."

In 1992, Mo got off to a slow start and actually wound up back at Pawtucket, before returning for good in the second half of the season. He was crushed by the demotion, saying later, "That night was one of the toughest in my life. I felt like quitting the game." Later, he added the demotion "was probably the lowest point of my caareer as an athlete."

After being sent down, Mo met his parents at a small hotel and they talked him into staying with his dream. "They lovingly put their arms around me and gently reminded me to believe in myself, just as they had done all along," Mo said. "They said I would get another chance if I worked hard and followed my dreams.

"By the end of our talk, I knew I'd make it back to Boston some day."

It was then Mo made the first real negative comments about an organization he would end up leaving—after a bumpy ride that included some off-field troubles and terrible contract battles. "It's not like the Red Sox are the end result of baseball for me," Mo said. "There are other teams ... There'll be two more teams next year (with expansion). (The Sox) have to decide what they're going to do ... I want to make the big leagues,and it may not be here."

It was with Boston, but the words had a ring to them that would come back to haunt the Red Sox.

Sent to the minors May 11, Mo was back in Boston June 22 (after hitting .282 with six homers in the minors). He would never return to the minor leagues again.

In 113 total games with the Red Sox that year, he batted .234, with 13 homers and 57 RBIs—making 15 errors at first base. Seven of those errors came on missed throws, including the Naehring throw Sept. 19 that led to all the trouble.

By the end of the 1992 season, Mo had played

Mo watches another ball leave the park. (AP/Wide World Photos)

in 210 big-league games. He had batted .244, with 17 homers, 89 RBIs, 110 strikeouts and 21 errors. He had not burst onto the major-league scene, and really did not give an adequate indication of the success that was to come.

There was a quick indication of what Mo would mean to the community, however. He was named Man of the Year by the BoSox Club—the Red Sox' booster group—for his growing involvement in the city. The Mo Vaughn Youth Center was making its debut and Mo made regular visits to a local elementary school.

On the field, the really good stuff would all start the next season—when Mo, a student of batting coach and guru Mike Easler, would just miss hitting .300, a mark he would reach five consecutive times in the future.

CHAPTER SIX 6

Making Some Noise

Mo's first full year in the major leagues did a lot to silence his critics. He hit .297, with 34 doubles, 29 homers and 101 RBIs. He was ninth in the American League in slugging percentage (.509) and 10th in on-base percentage (.390).

Opposing teams were starting to notice, too—Mo was tied for third in the league with 23 intentional walks. On July 8, Mo hit his first career grand slam, tagging Oakland's Todd Van Poppel.

He was also developing his special relationship

In 1994, Mo inspired images of Babe Ruth when he fulfilled his promise to hit a home run for a sick child. (AP/Wide World Photos)

with kids, working in the community and even doing a Babe Ruth act when he promised a sick child a home run and then delivered.

In Anaheim one weekend, Mo promised little Jason Leader a homer that night—and delivered. It was clear Mo was special.

The next year, in spring training, it was also clear that Mo was driven. No Florida R&R for this guy. "I'm kind of tough on myself in spring training because how you practice is how you're going to play when it really counts," he said before getting off to a blazing start, hitting .360 in April. He wound up at .310 with 26 homers and 82 RBIs—even more impressive considering a strike ended the baseball season with six weeks remaining.

Mo also received his second straight Thomas A. Yawkey Award (named in honor of the former Sox owner) as the Sox MVP—the honor given by the Boston Baseball Writers.

All that was just a warmup for 1995—when Mo would be the Most Valuable Player of the entire American League.

Mo takes the field at Fenway Park. (AP/Wide World Photos)

CHAPTER SEVEN

Mr. MVP

In 1993 and 1994, an abundance of All Star-caliber first baseman resulted in Toronto manager Cito Gaston leaving Mo off the American League All-Star team both years. He was deserving each time and was upset he didn't make it. Just as he had done with past disappointments, however, Mo was able to turn both All-Star snubs into a learning experience.

"It's like when I got sent down (in 1992)," he said when he did make it to his first All Star Game. "When I came back and finally started doing my job, I enjoyed it even more; Same thing here—not being here before, it will make it even more fun being here now.

"It's nice to be around those types of players. It's nice to be on that level with everybody who's great in the game. These are the same guys who beat you with the big hit late in the game during the season, or the guys who make the tough pitches to strike you out. This is the best, you want to be around the best."

Even though he struck out both times in his first All-Star appearance, it was clear Mo was becoming one of the best hitters in the game. He was getting more disciplined at the plate.

Yes, he would always strike out, but he was making it happen more under his terms. He was making all his hard work with Easler pay off—and when Easler was replaced before the start of the 1994 season by former Sox great Jim Rice, Mo was upset but never skipped a beat. He worked with Rice and was always getting advice from other great left-handed hitters around the game (he idolized Kirby Puckett and Cecil Fielder but they were right-handed). "I always wanted to be like Kirby Puckett," he once said. "I'd want Reggie Jackson's power, and Carlton Fisk's attitude and love of the game. But mostly, I'd want to hustle like Kirby Puckett."

In 1995, Mo did it all. He hit .308, belted 39 homers and drove in 126 runs. He hit 11 homers in May and went on to lead the major leagues with 74 road RBI. He then nipped Albert Belle in the closest MVP battle ever in what may have come down to the opinions of baseball writers about who was the nicer guy. Belle may have had slightly better numbers, but character is mentioned on the ballot—and there were few better than Mo, few worse than Belle in that category.

"To be considered MVP at the major-league

level is something that's tremendous," Mo said the day he won. "You hope you get a job every day, let alone this. This honor is definitely unbelievable. It probably hasn't hit me right now."

Mo did want to make it clear that what he did off the field was merely a cherry on top of his cake—that he didn't win the award because of it. His numbers were right there with Belle's, but there's no doubt the two personalities probably decided the race.

For Mo, winning the MVP award was just another step—another validation. He really didn't take it with that much enthusiasm—rather as an almost predictable result of the work he had put in and, yes, the pain he had suffered getting to that point.

"I never was that excited about the MVP," he said. "I never really talked about it. I didn't really think about it either way. But everyone started

Mo was the 1995 American League MVP. (AP/Wide World Photos)

bringing it up the last couple of days. I never really was thinking about it until everybody started talking about it."

Even though the award was announced in November, Belle had already gotten some revenge in the post-season the previous month. Mo went 0-for-14, with seven strikeouts, as the Red Sox lost three straight games to Belle's Cleveland Indians. Belle homered in the opener and drove in three runs in the series—Mo and slugging teammate Jose Canseco combined to go 0-for-27.

It was another obstacle that would help Mo Vaughn become an even better player.

CHAPTER EIGHT

Three Years Left in Boston

Mo would never rest on what he had already accomplished. He was already having contract troubles with the Red Sox and the marriage would eventually end.

In 1996, Mo hit .326 with career highs in homers (43) and RBIs (144). He also had 207 hits—truly a great year. He tied the Sox record for homers in April with eight and was on his way. He also received the B.A.T. (Baseball Assistance Team) Bart Giamatti Award for community service.

Mo throws out the runner as pitcher Dennis Eckersley looks on. (AP/Wide World Photos)

In 1997, Mo, upset the Red Sox allowed Roger Clemens to sign with Toronto, needed knee surgery in June that knocked him out of what should have been his third straight All Star appearance. He still hit .315 with 35 homers and 96 RBIs in 141 games.

Defensively, Mo was still making errors (his 15 led the league in 1996 and he made 14 the following season) but he was getting better. In 1998, Mo's final year with the Red Sox, Mo played under the cloud of his contract problems. He talked a little too much about his situation, but that's Mo—a player who wears his heart on his sleeve and always leaves it on the field. The pressure was there to fail, but Mo had seen pressure before.

He hit .337 in 1998, just missing the batting title—won by the Yankees' Bernie Williams on the final day of the season—and slugged 40 homers and drove in 115 runs. He cleared that magic 200-

Mo waves to the Fenway Park crowd from the back of a police horse after the Red Sox won the American League pennant. (AP/Wide World Photos)

hit mark with 205. Another injury forced him to rest through another All Star Game, but he still played 154 games—and he viewed his second 200-hit season as a great accomplishment. Remember, Mo weighs 230 pounds and doesn't get many infield hits. He also often hits against an infield shift with three infielders to the right of second base.

In 1998, Mo played his second—and final year—with another growing Red Sox name. Mo and prized young shortstop Nomar Garciaparra became a lethal 1-2 punch for a team that wound up going to the playoffs as the AL's wild-card team. This time, Mo erased the 1995 experience in a hurry by homering twice in the first game.

He hit .412 in the series and his Red Sox career ended when he was removed for a pinch runner in the eighth inning of the fourth and final game. Sox fans sensed they had seen the last of their home-grown talent and let him know he was appreciated.

During the season, the two sides had talked and Mo, seeing other things being taken care of by the Red Sox around him, said some things that showed his frustration. It was easy to tell he was frustrated—one day he thought he was staying, the next he was going.

In the end, it seemed the Sox didn't really want him—so he left.

"I knew it was going to come to this and I was prepared for it," Mo said. "I knew when Roger Clemens left I was going to leave here. I knew if they let a Hall of Famer get away they were going to let a Mo Vaughn go.

"Once the season started and I didn't have a contract, I knew it was over. Last year was almost like I was still here but at the same time I was gone. I have no regrets. I did what I had to do. I have no

Mo waits out an intentional walk. (AP/Wide World Photos)

hard feelings whatsoever against the Red Sox. They gave me my start, they helped my career.

"I just want to wish my teammates, (manager) Jimy Williams and the coaches well. I hope I made my teammates better players and better people and they will always be in my heart and in my mind. The most important thing for me is the friendships I made in that clubhouse and not being there with them is going to be hard."

There were many people who felt the Sox made up their minds to not offer Mo enough to stay after a drunk driving arrest on January 9, 1998 (he was later acquitted) but there were others who felt the team's mind was made up even before that. That theory was probably false because Mo was close to signing just months before the arrest—just before the Sox gave Pedro Martinez what was at the time the richest contract in baseball.

CHAPTER NINE

Hello Disneyland

The Angels sent Mo a letter just after the season letting him know they considered him special. To Mo, things like that mean the world. He was wanted, something he often felt wasn't the case during his years in Boston. The Sox had made him contract offers but they always seemed to be the kinds of bids a person had to refuse.

With the Angels, it was different—and there Mo was, ready to join his new team and start a new life at age 30.

Mo snags balls at batting practice. (AP/Wide World Photos)

"They saw some things in me I really didn't see myself," Mo said. "I appreciated that. You never know what people think about you on the other side. This is a team I always looked at as one to fear in the American League. I would never tell them that, I was trying to beat them."

His new manager, Terry Collins, didn't need much to convince him of Mo's talent on and off the field, but he did ask around, asking Mo's teammate, knuckleballer Tim Wakefield, about Mo. "He's the best," Collins said Wakefield told him. "I've known Tim for a long time. That's good enough for me.

"The signing of Mo Vaughn is an extraordinary event for our ballclub. Mo is one of those guys whose presence will have a profound effect on the players, the organization and the community. Our ownership has established its desire to take this team to the next level, and Mo is the type of individual who relishes that challenge."

Said Mo, "All I know is I'm just trying to bring a winning attitude to this club. They've got a great bunch of guys. I kind of just want to fit in and help their team."

Mo knew his time would come to exhibit those great leadership talents. "I'll try to push people to play well, believe in themselves," he said. "They've got a good bunch of guys on this ballclub. It's their clubhouse, they've been here longer than I have. We're all looking for the same thing. By midseason, I'll probably have something to say."

That was exactly the reason—along with his on-field ability—the Angels wanted to sign Vaughn.

"First and foremost is his ability on the field, and second to that but real close is his presence in the clubhouse and his presence on his ballclub," said Bavasi.

Four of his new teammates, including reliever

Troy Percival, attended the press confernce that welcomed Mo to the Angels. "There's no doubt he's consistently in the top five hitters in the league," said Percival. "He plays the game the right way."

Added pitcher Chuck Finley, "He's a wonderful addition to our club. Everybody around the league respects Mo, the way he plays. He's coming to a good team, he can only improve it. He'll blend in with the team easy. You're an outcast if you don't play hard."

Clearly, that's not a problem with Mo. Bavasi said he spoke to the Angels hitting coach about Mo and was told, "You need to get a guy who will say, 'Come on, get on my back, let's go.' That's the guy, that's just the way it is.

"You have to have watched how his teammates (in Boston) fed off him," added Bavasi "That's what he's there for. He's there for his teammates. He's there for the community."

Mo and John Valentin (left) congratulate each other after scoring two runs for the Red Sox. (AP/Wide World Photos)

CHAPTER TEN

Teammates Are Stunned

Naturally, the news that Mo was leaving was not well received by his Red Sox teammates.

"Holy cow," Pedro Martinez told the Boston Herald when reached at his home in the Dominican Republic. "I am really sad to see Mo go, because I really came over to the team because I thought Mo was going to be there all the time.

"He was one of the biggest influences for why I am in a Red Sox uniform. I have always been a huge fan of Mo. To me, this is a big loss."

Ironically, it was Martinez's new contract that kept Mo from signing a new deal with the Sox during the offseason between the 1997 and 1998 campaigns. It was even said Mo was on his way to Fenway Park to sign a new deal when he heard of Martinez' contract—and turned around and went home.

The news Mo was leaving meant the end of years and years of playing together for Mo and John Valentin, his teammate at Seton Hall and with the Sox. "I hate to see him go," Valentin said. "I don't know if it's a good move to let Mo Vaughn go. I was looking forward to him coming back. I guess there was a lot of anymosity there, and I don't know if Mo was willing to put it behind him. I'm actually very surprised about this, but you never know."

All summer, as Mo kept sensing he was going to leave, Valentin kept saying his buddy would stay. Even when Mo and the Sox announced the split,

Valentin held out hope things could be worked out. They couldn't.

"I wish him all the best," Valentin said. "I'm not going to be angry for him doing this. He's always wanted to be wanted. It's hard to say (if the Red Sox wanted him). I can easily say no, but I don't know if that's accurate. I'm sure they wanted him,but Mo hasn't always been nice to the organization."

Valentin then addressed the club's pursuit of Yankee star Bernie Williams, who eventually stayed in New York after talking to the Sox. "Bernie Williams is a very nice player, a very good player, but is he in the class of Mo Vaughn? I don't think so," Valentin said. "I'm not trying to shoot Williams down, but he's not in the class of Mo Vaughn. Is he going to lead like Mo Vaughn? I don't know. Is he going to hit 40 home runs like Mo Vaughn? I don't know. And a guy like Bernie Williams is going to get $100 million? I don't know if the Sox can afford Mo Vaughn—obviously they can't if they think he's only worth $60 million."

Mo Vaughn returns five years after graduating from Trinity Pawling School to speak to the students at a sports award banquet. (Trinity Pawling)

CHAPTER 11 ELEVEN

The Kids Will Miss Him

Mo did not relish leaving Boston. As he said when he signed with the Angels, he was going to Anaheim to "go to work." He was still living in Boston and would continue his work with the kids and with the youth center he built. Obviously, he would do the same type of work in Southern California, because that's his nature.

The man has a heart big enough to help both coasts, but there was still a feeling in Boston that Mo never should have left. "You see exactly what happens when people do the right thing," Mo said

Mo visits with kids at the Mo Vaughn Youth Development Center. (AP/Wide World Photos)

of the Angels—and against the Red Sox. "The only ones that get hurt are the fans and the players. Those are the ones who are suffering."

As he said, Mo will continue to help the kids in Boston—including his trips taking children to the Nutcracker ballet. The difference is he no longer will be a presence, which means it cannot be the same.

During his talks with the kids at the Mo Vaughn Youth Development Center in Dorchester, Massachusetts, Mo's message is basic—work hard and get what you want out of life. "I talk about work ethic, I talk about character, I talk about learning," he says. "I want to let young people see how hard work can be successful. Kids need to keep their minds open, not to feel peer pressure.

"I want them to see all different types of things, different types of attitudes and especially all different types of professions. A lot of kids think they're

Mo believes it's important for kids not to feel pressure. (AP/Wide World Photos)

failures if they're not an athlete or an entertainer and that's not true."

Mo helps them believe that. To him, he isn't doing any great or unusual thing by helping these kids grow up.

"If people want you around, then I think it's your job to be around," he says. "It's nothing that's very, very hard. I get along with people well. I like kids and I want to hear what they have to say. Everybody has something to say to them. People always have a plan of action for them without even asking them how they feel."

Jane Novotny, development director of St. Francis House, a Boston homeless shelter, may have said it best when she told the *Boston Herald*, "It's tough. I was not happy to read of his departure. He meant a great deal to us."

Mo meant a great deal to a lot of people in Boston and the surrounding areas. Even though he became an Angel, he promised to still be a part of the Boston scene.

Somehow, everyone knew it would never be the same. "He really helped the homeless," said Novotny. "He would stop by in the middle of the day to meet with our clients. He'd play dominoes, sign autographs. He really just reached out to make a difference in our lives."

That's something nobody can take away from him.

Mo has averaged 118 RBI over the past three seasons. (AP/Wide World Photos)

Mo stops to visit with a fan. (AP/Wide World Photos)

Mo Vaughn Quick Facts

Full Name: Maurice Samuel Vaughn

Team: Anaheim Angels

Hometown: Norwalk, Connecticut

Position: First Base

Jersey Number: 42

Bats: Left

Throws: Right

Height: 6-1

Weight: 240 pounds

Birthdate: December 15, 1967

1998 Highlight: Batted a career-high .337, second best average in American League

Stats Spotlight: Has averaged 40 home runs and 118 RBI over the last three seasons

Little-Known Fact: Mo Vaughn was a three-time All-American at Seton Hall University

Mo Vaughn's Professional Career

Year Club	AVG	G	AB	R	H	2B	3B	HR	RBI	BB	SO	SB
1991 Boston	.260	74	219	21	57	12	0	4	32	26	43	2
1992 Boston	.234	113	355	42	83	16	2	13	57	47	67	3
1993 Boston	.297	152	539	86	160	34	1	29	101	79	130	4
1994 Boston	.310	111	394	65	122	25	1	26	82	57	112	4
1995 Boston	.300	140	550	98	165	28	3	39	126*	68	150*	11
1996 Boston	.326	161	635	118	207	29	1	44	143	95	154	2
1997 Boston	.315	141	527	91	166	24	0	35	96	86	154	2
1998 Boston	.337	154	609	107	205	31	2	40	115	61	144	0
Career Totals	.304	1046	3828	628	1165	199	10	230	752	519	954	28
Postseason Totals	.226	7	31	3	7	2	0	2	7	2	12	0

* Denotes League Leader

Career Fielding Statistics

Year	Team	Posn	G	GS	TC	PO	A	E	DP	FLD%
1991	Boston	1B	49	47	410	378	26	6	43	.985
1992	Boston	1B	85	82	813	741	57	15	76	.982
1993	Boston	1B	131	130	1196	1110	70	16	104	.987
1994	Boston	1B	106	105	947	880	57	10	103	.989
1995	Boston	1B	138	138	1368	1262	95	11	128	.992
1996	Boston	1B	146	146	1296	1207	74	15	123	.988
1997	Boston	1B	131	131	1177	1088	75	14	117	.988
1998	Boston	1B	142	142	1277	1175	90	12	91	.991
Fielding Totals			928	921	8484	7841	544	99	785	.988
Post Season Fielding Ttls			7	7	63	57	6	0	3	1.000

1998 AL BA Leaders

Bernie Williams	.339
Mo Vaughn	**.337**
Albert Belle	.328
Eric Davis	.327
Derek Jeter	.324

1998 AL Slugging Pct.

Albert Belle	.655
Juan Gonzalez	.630
Ken Griffey Jr.	.611
Manny Ramirez	.599
Carlos Delgado	.592
Mo Vaughn	**.591**
Nomar Garciaparra	.584
Jim Thome	.584
Eric Davis	.582
Bernie Williams	.575

Mo hit .337 in 1998. (AP/Wide World Photos)

1998 AL Runs Leaders

1.	Derek Jeter	127
2.	Ray Durham	126
3.	Alex Rodriguez	123
4.	Ken Griffey Jr	120
5.	Chuck Knoblauch	117
15.	**Mo Vaughn**	**107**

1998 AL MVP Voting

Juan Gonzalez	357
Nomar Garciaparra	232
Derek Jeter	180
Mo Vaughn	**135**
Ken Griffey Jr.	135
Manny Ramirez	127
Bernie Williams	103

1998 AL BA Leaders

Bernie Williams	.339
Mo Vaughn	**.337**
Albert Belle	.328
Eric Davis	.327
Derek Jeter	.324

AL MVP Winners in the '90s

1998	Juan Gonzalez, Texas
1997	Ken Griffey Jr., Seattle
1996	Juan Gonzalez, Texas
1995	**Mo Vaughn, Boston**
1994	Frank Thomas, Chicago
1993	Frank Thomas, Chicago
1992	Dennis Eckersley, Oakland
1991	Cal Ripken, Baltimore
1990	Rickey Henderson, Oakland

1998 American League RBI Leaders

1.	Juan Gonzalez	157
2.	Albert Belle	152
3.	Ken Griffey Jr.	146
4.	Manny Ramirez	145
5.	Alex Rodriguez	124
12.	**Mo Vaughn**	**115**

1998 American League HR Leaders

1.	Ken Griffey Jr.	56
2.	Albert Belle	49
3.	Jose Canseco	46
4.	Juan Gonzalez	45
5.	Manny Ramirez	45
8.	**Mo Vaughn**	**40**

Active Career Slugging Percentage

1.	Frank Thomas	.584
2.	Albert Belle	.577
3.	Mark McGwire	.576
4.	Mike Piazza	.575
5.	Ken Griffey Jr.	.568
6.	Juan Gonzalez	.568
7.	Manny Ramirez	.558
8.	Barry Bonds	.556
9.	Nomar Garciaparra	.552
	Larry Walker	.552
10.	Jim Thome	.549
13.	**Mo Vaughn**	**.542**

Mo circles the bases after one of his 40 1998 homers.
(AP/Wide World Photos)

Active Career BA Leaders

1.	Tony Gwynn	.339
2.	Mike Piazza	.333
3.	Wade Boggs	.329
4.	Frank Thomas	.321
5.	Edgar Martinez	.318
6.	Alex Rodriguez	.313
7.	Kenny Lofton	.311
8.	Rusty Greer	.310
9.	Mark Grace	.310
10.	Nomar Garciaparra	.309
16.	**Mo Vaughn**	**.304**

Active Career OB % Leaders

Frank Thomas	.443
Edgar Martinez	.424
Wade Boggs	.416
Jeff Bagwell	.411
Barry Bonds	.411
Jim Thome	.409
Rickey Henderson	.404
John Olerud	.403
Mike Piazza	.396
Tim Salmon	.395
Mo Vaughn	**.394**

1998 AL Singles Leaders

Derek Jeter	151
Jose Offerman	143
Tom Goodwin	133
Mo Vaughn	**132**
Mike Caruso	132

1998 Hits Leaders

Alex Rodriguez	213
Mo Vaughn	**205**
Derek Jeter	203
Albert Belle	200
Nomar Garciaparra	195

Derek Jeter: The Yankee Kid

Author: Jack O'Connell
ISBN: 1-58261-043-6

In 1996 Derek burst onto the scene as one of the most promising young shortstops to hit the big leagues in a long time. His hitting prowess and ability to turn the double play have definitely fulfilled the early predictions of greatness.

A native of Kalamazoo, MI, Jeter has remained well grounded. He patiently signs autographs and takes time to talk to the young fans who will be eager to read more about him in this book.

Bernie Williams: Quiet Superstar

Author: Kevin Kernan
ISBN: 1-58261-044-4

Bernie Williams, a guitar-strumming native of Puerto Rico, is not only popular with his teammates, but is considered by top team officials to be the heir to DiMaggio and Mantle fame.

He draws frequent comparisons to Roberto Clemente, perhaps the greatest player ever from Puerto Rico. Like Clemente, Williams is humble, unassuming, and carries himself with quiet dignity. Also like Clemente, he plays with rare determination and a special elegance. He's married, and serves as a role model not only for his three children, but for his young fans here and in Puerto Rico.

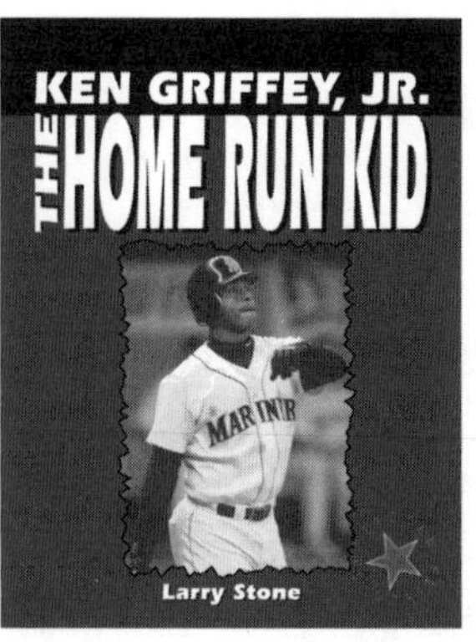

Ken Griffey, Jr.: The Home Run Kid

Author: Larry Stone

ISBN: 1-58261-041-x

Capable of hitting majestic home runs, making breathtaking catches, and speeding around the bases to beat the tag by a split second, Ken Griffey, Jr. is baseball's Michael Jordan. Amazingly, Ken reached the Major Leagues at age 19, made his first All-Star team at 20, and produced his first 100 RBI season at 21.

The son of Ken Griffey, Sr., Ken is part of the only father-son combination to play in the same outfield together in the same game, and, like Barry Bonds, he's a famous son who turned out to be a better player than his father.

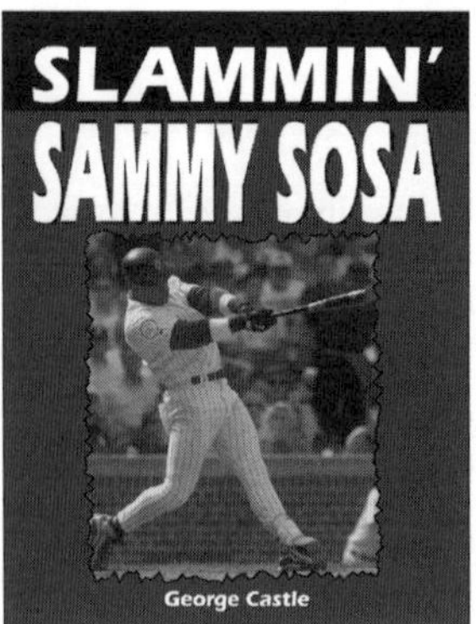

Sammy Sosa: Slammin' Sammy

Author: George Castle

ISBN: 1-58261-029-0

1998 was a break-out year for Sammy as he amassed 66 home runs, led the Chicago Cubs into the playoffs and finished the year with baseball's ultimate individual honor, MVP.

When the national spotlight was shone on Sammy during his home run chase with Mark McGwire, America got to see what a special person he is. His infectious good humor and kind heart have made him a role model across the country.

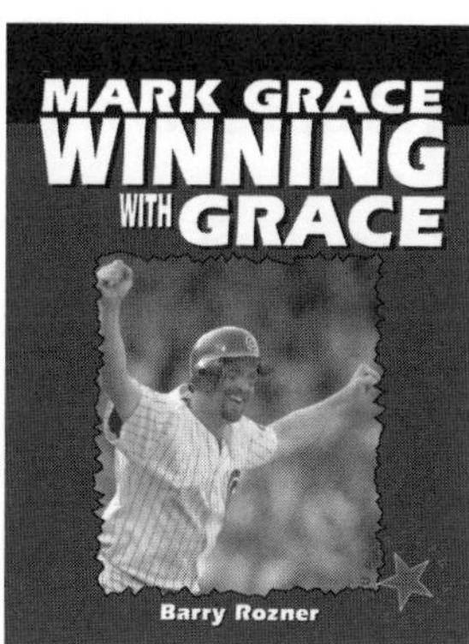

Mark Grace: Winning with Grace

Author: Barry Rozner

ISBN: 1-58261-056-8

This southern California native and San Diego State alumnus has been playing baseball in the windy city for nearly fifteen years. Apparently the cold hasn't affected his game. Mark is an all-around player who can hit to all fields and play great defense.

Mark's outgoing personality has allowed him to evolve into one of Chicago's favorite sons. He is also community minded and some of his favorite charities include the Leukemia Society of America and Easter Seals.

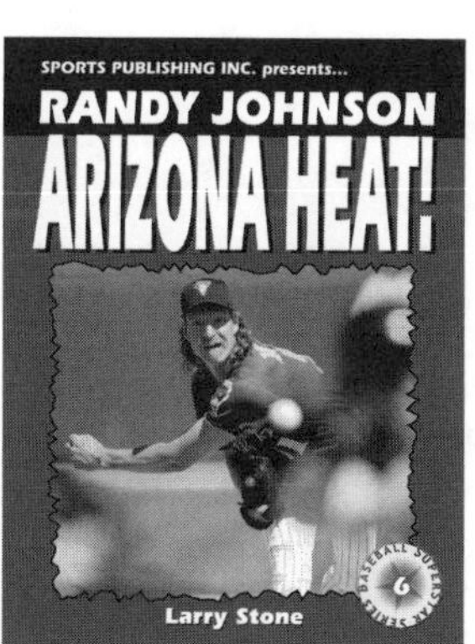

Randy Johnson: Arizona Heat!

Author: Larry Stone

ISBN: 1-58261-042-8

One of the hardest throwing pitchers in the Major Leagues, and, at 6'10" the tallest, the towering figure of Randy Johnson on the mound is an imposing sight which strikes fear into the hearts of even the most determined opposing batters.

Perhaps the most amazing thing about Randy is his consistency in recording strikeouts. He is one of only four pitchers to lead the league in strikeouts for four consecutive seasons. With his recent signing with the Diamondbacks, his career has been rejuvenated and he shows no signs of slowing down.

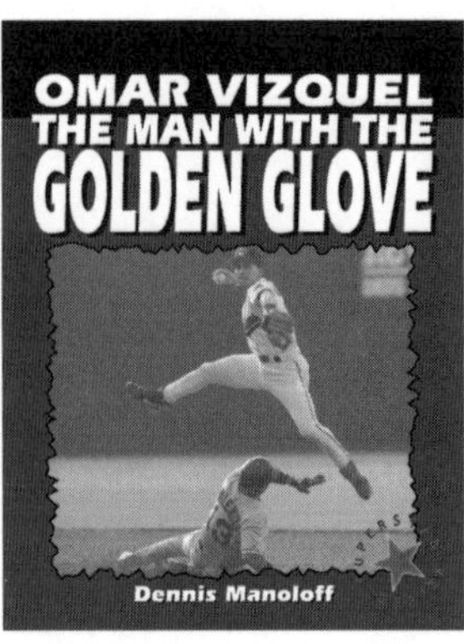

Omar Vizquel: The Man with the Golden Glove

Author: Dennis Manoloff

ISBN: 1-58261-045-2

Omar has a career fielding percentage of .982 which is the highest career fielding percentage for any shortstop with at least 1,000 games played.

Omar is a long way from his hometown of Caracas, Venezuela, but his talents as a shortstop put him at an even greater distance from his peers while he is on the field.

Pedro Martinez: Throwing Strikes

Author: Mike Shalin

ISBN: 1-58261-047-9

The 1997 National League Cy Young Award winner is always teased because of his boyish looks. He's sometimes mistaken for the batboy, but his curve ball and slider leave little doubt that he's one of the premier pitchers in the American League.

It is fitting that Martinez is pitching in Boston, where the passion for baseball runs as high as it does in his native Dominican Republic.

Nomar Garciaparra: High 5!

Author: Mike Shalin

ISBN: 1-58261-053-3

An All-American at Georgia Tech, a star on the 1992 U.S. Olympic Team, the twelfth overall pick in the 1994 draft, and the 1997 American League Rookie of the Year, Garciaparra has exemplified excellence on every level.

At shortstop, he'll glide deep into the hole, stab a sharply hit grounder, then throw out an opponent on the run. At the plate, he'll uncoil his body and deliver a clutch double or game-winning homer. Nomar is one of the game's most complete players.

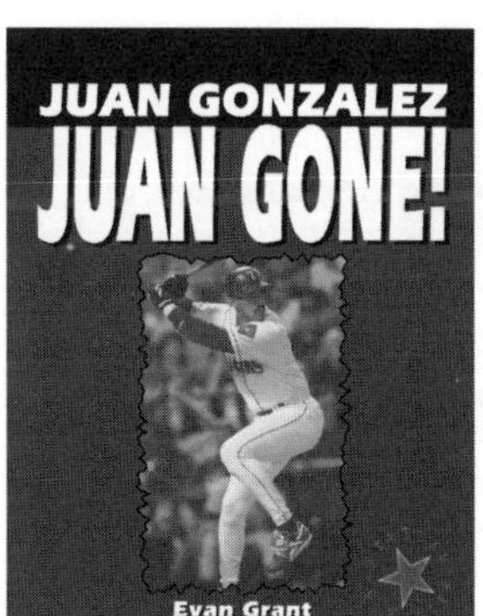

Juan Gonzalez: Juan Gone!

Author: Evan Grant

ISBN: 1-58261-048-7

One of the most prodigious and feared sluggers in the major leagues, Gonzalez was a two-time home run king by the time he was 24 years old.

After having something of a personal crisis in 1996, the Puerto Rican redirected his priorities and now says baseball is the third most important thing in his life after God and family.

Mo Vaughn: Angel on a Mission

Author: Mike Shalin
ISBN: 1-58261-046-0

Growing up in Connecticut, this Angels slugger learned the difference between right and wrong and the value of honesty and integrity from his parents early on, lessons that have stayed with him his whole life.

This former American League MVP was so active in Boston charities and youth programs that he quickly became one of the most popular players ever to don the Red Sox uniform.

Mo will be a welcome addition to the Angels line-up and the Anaheim community.

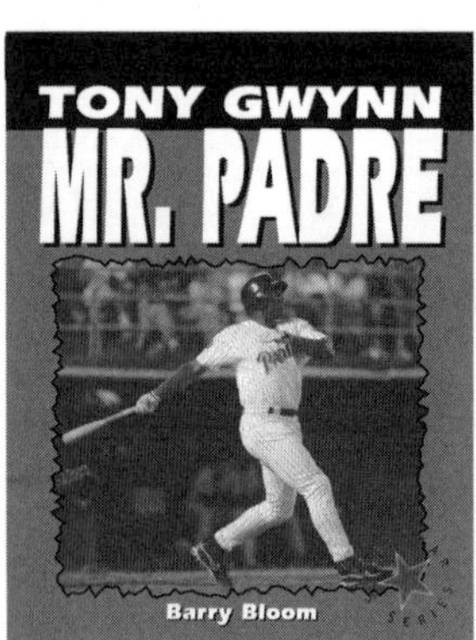

Tony Gwynn: Mr. Padre

Author: Barry Bloom
ISBN: 1-58261-049-5

Tony is regarded as one of the greatest hitters of all-time. He is one of only three hitters in baseball history to win eight batting titles (the others: Ty Cobb and Honus Wagner).

In 1995 he won the Branch Rickey Award for Community Service by a major leaguer. He is unfailingly humble and always accessible, and he holds the game in deep respect. A throwback to an earlier era, Gwynn makes hitting look effortless, but no one works harder at his craft.

Kevin Brown:
That's Kevin with a "K"

Author: Jacqueline Salman

ISBN: 1-58261-050-9

Kevin was born in McIntyre, Georgia and played college baseball for Georgia Tech. Since then he has become one of baseball's most dominant pitchers and when on top of his game, he is virtually unhittable.

Kevin transformed the Florida Marlins and San Diego Padres into World Series contenders in consecutive seasons, and now he takes his winning attitude and talent to the Los Angeles Dodgers.

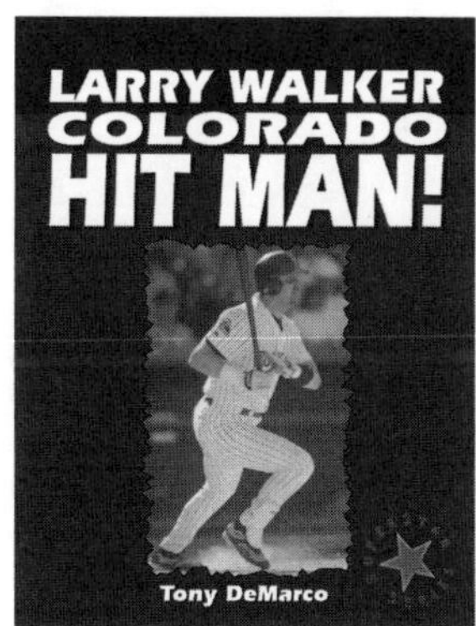

Larry Walker:
Colorado Hit Man!

Author: Tony DeMarco

ISBN: 1-58261-052-5

Growing up in Canada, Larry had his sights set on being a hockey player. He was a skater, not a slugger, but when a junior league hockey coach left him off the team in favor of his nephew, it was hockey's loss and baseball's gain.

Although the Rockies' star is known mostly for his hitting, he has won three Gold Glove awards, and has worked hard to turn himself into a complete, all-around ballplayer. Larry became the first Canadian to win the MVP award.

Sandy and Roberto Alomar: Baseball Brothers

Author: Barry Bloom

ISBN: 1-58261-054-1

Sandy and Roberto Alomar are not just famous baseball brothers they are also famous baseball sons. Sandy Alomar, Sr. played in the major leagues fourteen seasons and later went into management. His two baseball sons have made names for themselves and have appeared in multiple All-Star games.

With Roberto joining Sandy in Cleveland, the Indians look to be a front-running contender in the American League Central.

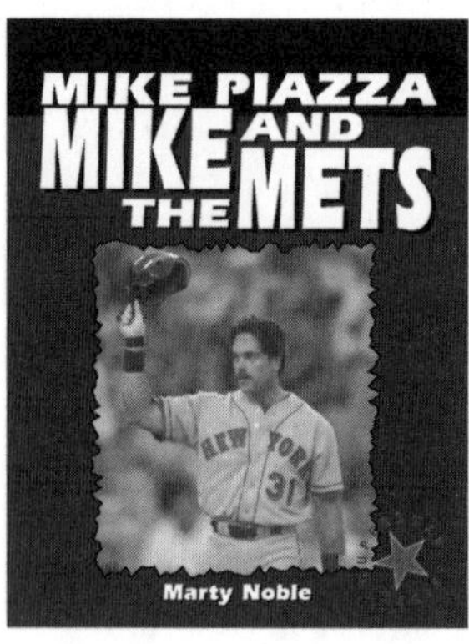

Mike Piazza: Mike and the Mets

Author: Marty Noble

ISBN: 1-58261-051-7

A total of 1,389 players were selected ahead of Mike Piazza in the 1988 draft, who wasn't picked until the 62nd round, and then only because Tommy Lasorda urged the Dodgers to take him as a favor to his friend Vince Piazza, Mike's father.

Named in the same breath with great catchers of another era like Bench, Dickey and Berra, Mike has proved the validity of his father's constant reminder "If you work hard, dreams do come true."

Curt Schilling: Phillie Phire!

Author: Paul Hagen

ISBN: 1-58261-055-x

Born in Anchorage, Alaska, Schilling has found a warm reception from the Philadelphia Phillies faithful. He has amassed 300+ strikeouts in the past two seasons and even holds the National League record for most strikeouts by a right handed pitcher at 319.

This book tells of the difficulties Curt faced being traded several times as a young player, and how he has been able to deal with off-the-field problems.

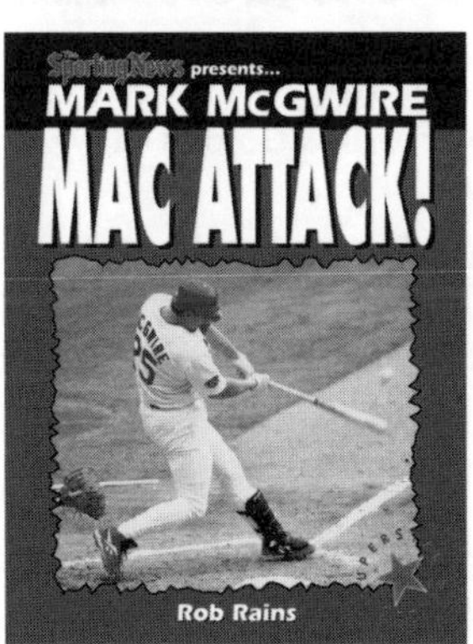

Mark McGwire: Mac Attack!

Author: Rob Rains

ISBN: 1-58261-004-5

Mac Attack! describes how McGwire overcame poor eyesight and various injuries to become one of the most revered hitters in baseball today. He quickly has become a legendary figure in St. Louis, the home to baseball legends such as Stan Musial, Lou Brock, Bob Gibson, Red Schoendienst and Ozzie Smith. McGwire thought about being a police officer growing up, but he hit a home run in his first Little League at-bat and the rest is history.

Roger Clemens: Rocket Man!

Author: Kevin Kernan

ISBN: 1-58261-128-9

Alex Rodriguez: A-plus Shortstop

ISBN: 1-58261-104-1